1 LET'S GO

4th Edition

WORKBOOK

R. Nakata

K. Frazier

B. Hoskins

J. McGasko

OXFORD

UNIVERSITY PRESS

OXFORD
UNIVERSITY PRESS

198 Madison Avenue
New York, NY 10016 USA

Great Clarendon Street, Oxford, OX2 6DP, United Kingdom

Oxford University Press is a department of the University of Oxford.
It furthers the University's objective of excellence in research, scholarship,
and education by publishing worldwide. Oxford is a registered trade
mark of Oxford University Press in the UK and in certain other countries

General Manager, American ELT: Laura Pearson
Executive Publishing Manager: Shelagh Speers
Senior Managing Editor: Anne Stribling
Project Editor: June Schwartz
Art, Design, and Production Director: Susan Sanguily
Design Manager: Lisa Donovan
Designer: Sangeeta E. Ramcharan
Electronic Production Manager: Julie Armstrong
Production Artist: Elissa Santos
Image Manager: Trisha Masterson
Image Editor: Joe Kassner
Production Coordinator: Hila Ratzabi
Senior Manufacturing Controller: Eve Wong

ISBN: 978 0 19 464320 7

Printed in China

This book is printed on paper from certified and well-managed sources

ACKNOWLEDGEMENTS

The authors and publisher are grateful to those who have given permission to reproduce the following extracts and adaptations of copyright material:

Illustrations by: Bernard Adnet: 26(t), 62(tl, tr, 3b, 3b, 4a) ; Fian Arroyo: 6, 22, 23, 37; Hector Borlasca: 34(t); Nancy Gayle Carlson: 39(b), 50, 75, 76, 77, 78, 79, 80; Mike Dammer: 12(b); Bob Depew: 48, 49, 58, 59, 62(1a, 1b, 3a), 68, 74(t); Mena Dolobowsky: 7, 9, 10, 17, 18, 27, 28, 35, 36, 45, 46, 53, 54, 63, 64, 71, 72; Liz Dubois: 32, 65(b); Elizabeth Dulemba: 16(t), 62(tc); Michael Garland: 8(t), 52(b); Daniel Griffo: cats on pages 3, 4, 6, 8, 11, 12, 14, 16, 21, 22, 24, 26, 29, 30, 32, 34, 39, 40, 42, 44, 47, 48, 50, 52, 57, 58, 60, 62, 65, 66, 68, 70; John Hom/AA Reps Inc.: 3, 11, 21, 29(t), 39(t), 47(t), 57(t), 65(t); Karen Lee: 69; KE Lewis: 47(b), 66, 67, 73; Colleen Madden: 44(t); Dana Regan: 20, 31, 38; Mary Rojas: 29(b), 33, 57(b); Janet Skiles: 34(b), 42, 43(t), 44(b), 55, 56, 70(b); Kristin Varner: 4, 8(b), 12(b), 13, 15, 19, 24, 25(t), 26(b), 40, 41, 51; Curt Walstead: 75(tl); Jason Wolff: 5, 25(b), 30, 43(b), 52(t), 60, 61, 74(b); Necdet Yilmaz: 70(t).

Text Design: Molly K. Scanlon
Cover Design: Debbie Lofaso
Cover Illustrator: Daniel Griffo

Unit 1 Things for School

Let's Talk

A Read and trace.

Hello. I'm Scott.

What's your name?

My name is Kate.

B Trace and write.

1. What's your name?

   I'm Jenny.

2. What is =

3. I am =

Let's Learn

A Check.

1.

- ☐ a book
- ☑ a pencil

2.

- ☐ a chair
- ☐ a desk

3.

- ☐ a ruler
- ☐ an eraser

4.

- ☐ a bag
- ☐ a pen

B Trace and match.

1. It is a bag. •
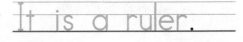

2. It is a ruler. •

•

3. It is a desk. •
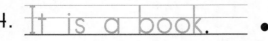
•

4. It is a book. •
•

C Read and write.

1.

It's a ruler.

2.

_It's_ _____ _._

3.

_____ .

4.

_____ .

D Match.

1.

•

• What's this?
It's an eraser.

2.

•

• What's this?
It's a pencil.

3.

•

• What's this?
It's a pen.

Let's Learn More

A Trace.

1. a marker

2. a poster

3. a globe

4. a table

5. a wastebasket

Hello

6. a board

B Trace and write.

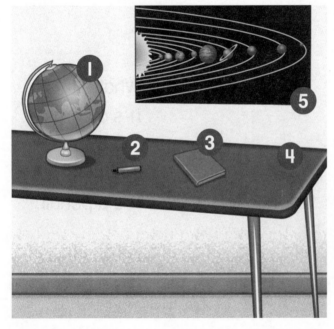

1. This is a globe.

2. _____.

3. _____.

4. _____.

5. _____.

table
book
globe
marker
poster

C Unscramble, write, and circle.

1. this a Is marker

Is this _____ ?

(Yes, it is.)
No, it isn't.
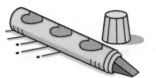

2. this Is crayon a

_____ ?

Yes, it is.
No, it isn't.

3. poster a Is this

_____ ?

Yes, it is.
No, it isn't.

4. Is wastebasket this a

_____ ?

Yes, it is.
No, it isn't.

D Match.

1. Take out your book. •

2. Open your book. •

3. Close your book. •

4. Put away your book. •

Let's Read

Phonics

A Match.

1. 
2. 
3. 
4. 
5. 
6. 

- bird
- peach
- ball
- boy
- pencil
- pink

Bb

Pp

B Write.

1. Bb

ball

2. Pp

peach

✓ Parent's signature: ______

At the Park

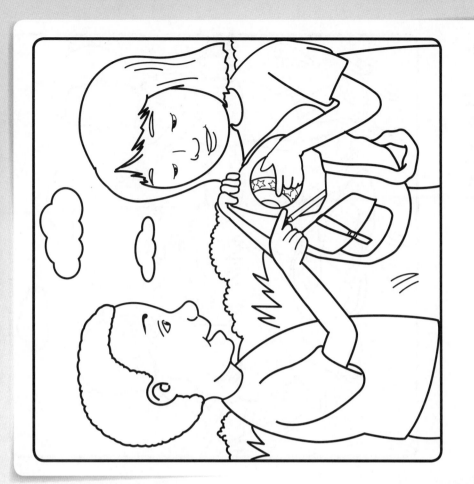

What's this?

No, it isn't.
It's a peach.

It's a ball.

Is this a ball?

A Read and trace.

Hi! How are you?

I'm fine. Thank you.

B Read and write.

I'm   How are you?   Hi   great

, how are you?

I'm _____ ?

_____ OK.

Let's Learn

A Unscramble, match, and color.

1. clabk   <u>black</u> •

2. regano   _____ •

3. energ   _____ •

4. weloly   _____ •

5. worbn   _____ •

• yellow

• brown

• black

• green

• orange

B Look and write.

1. <u>It's pink</u>.

2. _____.

3. _____.

4. _____.

C Read, circle, and color.

b = brown	o = orange	r = red
p = purple	g = green	y = yellow

1.  What color is this?
(It's red.)
It's yellow.

2.  What color is this?
It's yellow.
It's brown.

3.  What color is this?
It's green.
It's purple.

4.  What color is this?
It's green.
It's orange.

5.  What color is this?
It's red.
It's brown.

6.  What color is this?
It's purple.
It's orange.

D Trace, write, and color.

1.

What color is this?

It's pink.

2.

What color   ?

It's   .

3.

What   ?

            .

Let's Learn More

A Trace and match.

1. a diamond
2. a circle
3. a triangle
4. a heart
5. a square
6. a rectangle

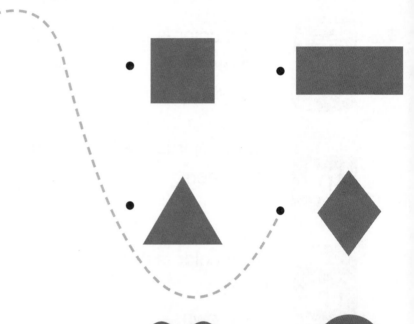

B Read and check.

	★	■	⬭	▭	◆
1. This is a rectangle.				✓	
2. This is an oval.					
3. This is a diamond.					
4. This is a star.					
5. This is a square.					

C Look and circle.

1.  Is this a triangle?
   (Yes, it is.)
   No, it isn't.

2.  Is this a heart?
   Yes, it is.
   No, it isn't.

3.  Is this a star?
   Yes, it is.
   No, it isn't.

4.  Is this a rectangle?
   Yes, it is.
   No, it isn't.

5.  Is this a diamond?
   Yes, it is.
   No, it isn't.

6.  Is this a circle?
   Yes, it is.
   No, it isn't.

D Trace and write.

1.
2.
3.
4.

Is this yellow?

Yes, it is.

_____ this a star?

No, _____. It's a _____.

_____ purple?

_____, _____. It's _____.

_____ rectangle?

_____, _____.

Phonics

A Match and trace.

1.

2.

3.

4.

5.

6.

Gg

Cc

- cow
- gate
- cat
- coat
- goat
- girl

B Write.

1. Cc

cow

2. Gg

gate

✓ Parent's signature: _____

This is my blue coat.
This is a green gate.

Oh, no!
Is this my blue coat?

This is a brown cow.
This is a black cat.

This is a white goat.

Let's Review ✓

A Read and match.

1. What's this?

• ⸺⸺⸺ • It's black.

2. Is this a diamond?

• • It's a globe.

3. What color is this?

• • No, it isn't. It's a circle.

4. Is this a star?

• • Yes, it is.

B Circle and color.

1. This is a black marker.

2. This is a green triangle.

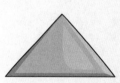

3. This is a blue diamond.

4. This is a red table.

C Look and check.

What's in the bag?

☑ a pencil   ☐ a crayon
☐ a book   ☐ a pen
☐ a map   ☐ a poster
☐ a notebook   ☐ a globe
☐ a ruler   ☐ an eraser

D Match.

1. Put away your book. •

2. Draw a picture. •

3. Open your book. •

4. Put away your pencil. •

5. Take out your book. •

✓ Parent's signature:_____

Let's Talk

A Trace and write.

| Hello | This | play | friend |

Hi, Scott. _____ is my _____ , Sarah.

_____ , Sarah.

Hi, Scott. Let's _____ !

B Read and number.

☐ Hi, Andy. Let's play!

☐ Hello, Sarah.

1 Hi, Andy. This is my friend, Sarah.

Let's Learn

A Write.

crayon	pencil case	crayons
markers	notebooks	marker

1.  pencil case

2. markers

3. _____

4.  _____

5. _____

6. _____

B Read, draw, and color.

1. Draw 5 green notebooks.

2. Draw 1 red table.
   Draw 4 blue pencil cases.

C Look and circle.

1. One crayon.
   (Ten crayons.)

2. One pencil case.
   Twelve pencil cases.

3. One marker.
   Eight markers.

4. One notebook.
   Ten notebooks.

D Write and check.

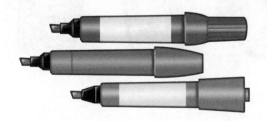

1. How many markers?

   ☑ Three markers.
   ☐ Four markers.

2. How many _____?

   ☐ Two pencils.
   ☐ Three pencils.

3. _____?

   ☐ Five notebooks.
   ☐ Seven notebooks.

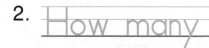

4. _____?

   ☐ Eight crayons.
   ☐ Ten crayons.

Let's Learn More

A Read and circle.

1. CDs

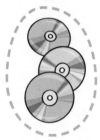  

2. a cell phone

3. computers

 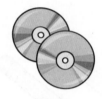 

4. a video game

B Look and check.

1.

- ☐ It's a pencil case.
- ☑ They're pencil cases.

2.

- ☐ It's a computer.
- ☐ They're computers.

3.

- ☐ It's a video game.
- ☐ They're video games.

4.

- ☐ It's a cell phone.
- ☐ They're cell phones.

C Trace, write, and match.

1. What are these?

2. What's this?

3. _____ ?

4. _____ ?

- It's a video game.

- It's a cell phone.

- They're CDs.

- They're computers.

D Trace and write.

Point	Find	Count

1. 1, 2, 3, 4 . . .

Count the books.

2. 1, 2, 3 . . .

_____ the video games.

3.

_____ to the computer.

4.

_____ the video games.

Let's Read

Phonics

A Trace and match.

1. desk

2. tiger

3. two

4. duck

5. door

6. toys

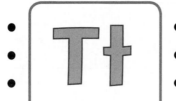

B Write.

1. Dd

duck

2. Tt

tiger

✓ Parent's signature:

At the Toy Store

Look at the toys!

SALE

Two ducks!

They're tigers.

How many ducks?

Unit 4 People at Home

Let's Talk

A Read and number.

 It's nice to meet you, Andy.

 | I | Hi, Mom! This is my friend, Andy.

 It's nice to meet you, too.

B Trace and write.

1.  This is my mother.

2.  This is _____.

   | father |
   | mother |
   | sister |
   | brother |

3.  _____.

4.  _____.

Let's Learn

A Trace and write.

baby sister
mother
grandfather
father
brother
grandmother

1. mother

2. _____

3. _____

4. _____

5. _____

6. _____

B Circle.

1.    (he)
    she

2.    he
    she

3.    he
    she

C Read and match.

1. grandmother •

2. brother •

3. baby sister •

4. grandfather •

D Read, write, and circle.

1. Who's she?

   She's my sister.

2. _____ he?

   He's my father.

3. _____ ?

   She's my mother.

4. _____ ?

   She's my grandmother.

Let's Learn More

A Trace and match.

1. young    tall

2. short   old

3. pretty    handsome

B Unscramble and write.

1. horts

He's short.

2. yetrtp

She's _____.

3. dol

_____.

4. ongyu

_____.

C Trace and write.

1.

Is she short?

Yes, she is.

2.

Is he tall?

No, he isn't.

3.

_____ he young?

Yes, _____.

4.

_____ tall?

_____.

D Look and circle.

1.

a. Read a book.
b. Count to ten.

2.

a. Say the alphabet.
b. Write the word.

3.

a. Say the alphabet.
b. Count to ten.

4.

a. Write the word.
b. Say the alphabet.

Phonics

A Unscramble and write.

Aa

1. pac

cap

2. gab

_____

3. tac

_____

4. peapl

_____

B Look and check.

1.  ☑ cap
☐ coat

2.   ☐ goat
☐ apple

3.  ☐ gate
☐ bag

4.  ☐ cat
☐ cap

✓ Parent's signature: _____

Let's Go to the Park

Is this your cat?
Yes, it is.

Who's he?
He's my brother!

This is my bag.
This is my cap.

Look at the apples!

Let's Review ✓

A Look and write.

1. What are these?

They're cell phones.

2. What is this?

It's _____ .

3. What are these?

_____ .

B Read and write.

1. Who's he?

   He's my brother.

2. _____ ?

   They're cell phones.

3. _____ ?

   It's a computer.

4. _____ ?

   She's my mother.

Who's she
Who's he
What are these
What's this

C Trace and write.

1. Who's he?

> grandfather
> old

He's my _____ .

He's _____ .

2. Who's she?

> mother
> pretty

She's _____ .

_____ .

_____ .

D Look and circle.

1.

(tall)　　short

2.

handsome　　pretty

3.

sister　　mother

4.

baby sister　　brother

5.

young　　old

6.

brother　　father

✓ Parent's signature:_____

Let's Talk

A Read and write.

| you | How old | birthday | seven | Thank | is |

1.

Happy birthday, Jenny! ___ are you?

I'm ___ years old.

2.

This ___ for ___.

___ you!

B Write and draw.

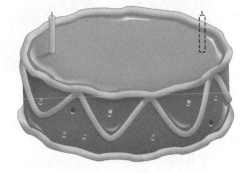

1. I'm six years old.

2. I'm ___.

Let's Learn

A Read and match.

1. a baseball •

2. a robot •

3. a bat •

4. a car •

5. a doll •

6. a puzzle •

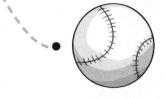

B Look and circle.

1. It's a   kite. / (bat.)

2. It's a   baseball. / doll.

3. It's a   puzzle. / bicycle.

4. It's a   yo-yo. / jump rope.

C Write and check.

1. What is it?
   - ☐ It's a robot.
   - ✓ It's a puzzle.
   - ☐ I don't know.

2. What ____?
   - ☐ It's a bicycle.
   - ☐ It's a yo-yo.
   - ☐ I don't know.

3. ____?
   - ☐ It's a doll.
   - ☐ It's a car.
   - ☐ I don't know.

4. ____?
   - ☐ It's a jump rope.
   - ☐ It's a ball.
   - ☐ I don't know.

D Write.

1. What is it?

   It's a kite.

2. What ____?

   It's ____.

3. ____?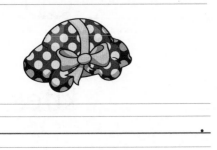

   ____.

4. ____?

   ____.

Let's Learn More

A Trace and circle.

1. big

2. little

3. long

4. short

5. round

6. square

B Circle and write.

1. (long)
   short

   It's a long jump rope.

2. big
   little

   It's a   bicycle.

3. round
   square

   It's a   CD.

4. new
   old

   It's an   kite.

C Read and check.

1. Is it a long pencil case?

☑ Yes, it is.

☐ No, it isn't. It's a short pencil case.

2. Is it an old video game?

☐ Yes, it is.

☐ No, it isn't. It's a new video game.

3. Is it an old bicycle?

☐ Yes, it is.

☐ No, it isn't. It's a new bicycle.

D Trace and match.

1. jump rope

2. catch a ball

3. ride a bicycle

4. throw a ball

Phonics

A Write.

Ee

  egg

 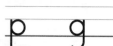 p ___ g

 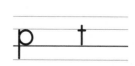 p ___ t

 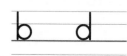 b ___ d

B Match.

1. pet •

2. peg •

3. bed •

4. egg •

✓ Parent's signature:_____

At Home

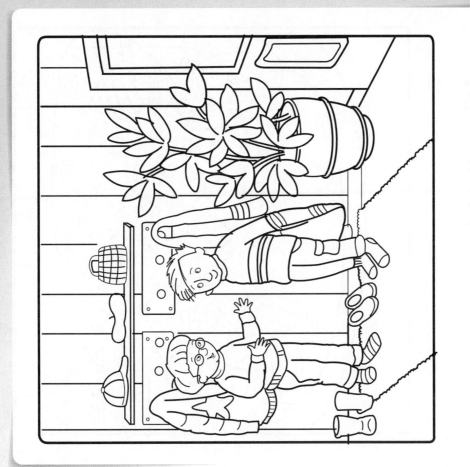

Put your coat on a peg.

I like eggs!

This is my pet.
It's a cat.

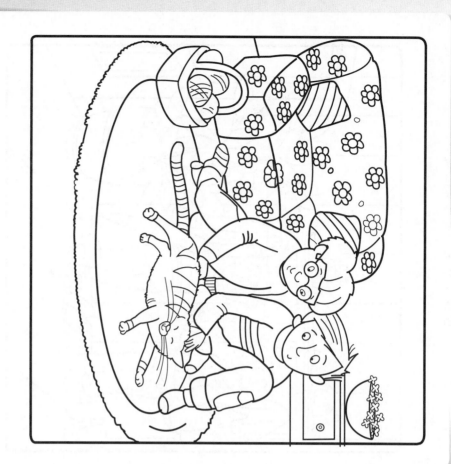

Is this an egg?
Yes, it is.

Unit 6 Outdoors

Let's Talk

A Trace and match.

1. windy
2. sunny
3. snowy
4. cloudy
5. rainy

B Write.

How is the weather?

1.  It's snowy today.

2.  It's _____ today.

3.  _____ today.

4.  _____ .

| sunny |
| rainy |
| cloudy |
| snowy |

Let's Learn

A Write and match.

1. <u>a puddle</u>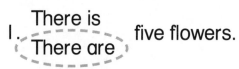

2. _____

3. _____

4. _____

• <u>puddles</u>

a puddle
puddles
a flower
flowers
a cloud
clouds
a tree
trees

B Read and circle.

1. There is
(There are) five flowers.

2. There is
There are one tree.

3. There is
There are three clouds.

4. There is
There are one puddle.

C Count and write.

1. There are five flowers.

2. There's one _____.

3. _____.

4. _____.

D Count and write.

1. How many books are there?
   There are three books.

2. _____ pens are there?
   _____.

3. _____ computers _____?
   There's _____.

4. _____?
   _____ erasers.

Let's Learn More

A Circle.

1.

in
(on)

2.
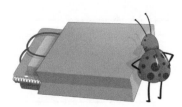
under
by

3.

in
by

4.

on
under

B Trace and write.

1.
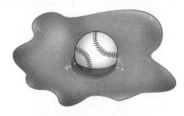
Where's the baseball?
It's in the puddle.

2.

are the flowers?
They're   the table.

3.

the bat?
the tree.

4.

the jump rope?
the table.

C Read and write.

| by | in | on | under |

1. Where's the book?

It's _____ the bag.

2. Where are the balls?

They're _____ the bag.

3. Where's the bicycle?

It's _____ the table.

4. Where are the dolls?

They're _____ the table.

D Look and write.

1.
Put the baseball _____ the table.

2.
Put the bat _____ the baseball.

3.
_____ the bag.

4.
_____ the tree.

Let's Read

A Circle.

1.

(p)	a	(t)
b	(i)	g
b	e	d

2.
t	a	b
p	i	t
b	e	g

3.

p	e	g
b	e	d
d	i	d

B Match.

1. pit ●

2. bib ●

3. igloo ●

4. big ●

In the Snow

It's snowy.
Let's make an igloo.

Let's play!

These are big squares.
This is a big pit.

This is the baby.
This is a bib.

Let's Review ✓

A Read and write.

> Where are the flowers   How many flowers are there
> What is it   Where's the book   Is it a big box

1. <u>What is it?</u> _____

   It's a short pencil.

2. _____ ?

   There are five flowers.

3. _____ ?

   It's in the bag.

4. _____ ?

   They're next to the tree.

5. _____ ?

   No, it isn't. It's a little box.

B Write.

in   on   under   by

1. The cat is in the bag.

2. The cat is _____ .

3. _____ .

4. _____ .

C Look and write.

three   two   four   one

1. How many puzzles are there?

   There are two puzzles.

2. How many clouds are there?

   There are _____ .

3. How many dolls are there?

   There's _____ .

4. How many puddles are there?

   _____ .

✓ Parent's
signature: _____

Unit 7 Food

Let's Talk

A Write.

> hungry   thirsty

1.

   I'm hungry.

2.

   I'm _____.

3.

   _____.

4.

   _____.

B Trace and write.

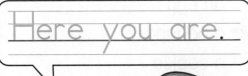

Here you are.

> You're welcome.
> Thank you.
> Here you are.

Parent's signature: _____

Let's Learn

A Write.

1.
2.
3.
4.

S	A	N	D	W	I	C	H
					G		

		L		D		

			N	A	N	A

5. I'm thirsty. I want a _____.

B Look and circle.

1. What do you want?

(a robot)
a yo-yo
a doll

2. What do you want?

an egg
a banana
a cookie

3. What do you want?

a salad
a soda
a sandwich

4. What do you want?

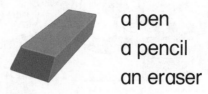

a pen
a pencil
an eraser

C Trace, write, and circle.

1. What do you want?

I want an egg.

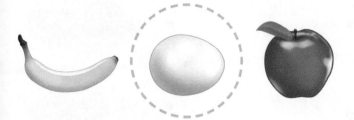

2. What do _____?

I want a soda.

3. _____?

I want a sandwich.

4. _____?

I want a banana.

D Read and circle.

What do you want?

1. I want a banana and an orange.

2. I want a sandwich and a salad.

3. I want an orange and a banana.

4. I want a milkshake and a cookie.

Let's Learn More

A Unscramble, write, and match.

1. cie samerc   ice cream

2. zizap

3. cire

4. cichekn

B Write.

1.    I want cake.

I don't want bread.

2. 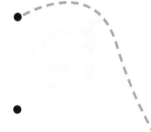   I   fish.

3.

C Read and circle.

1.  Do you want bread?
Yes, I do.
No, I don't.

2.  Do you want pizza?
Yes, I do.
No, I don't.

3.  Do you want cake?
Yes, I do.
No, I don't.

4.  Do you want chicken?
Yes, I do.
No, I don't.

D Trace and match.

1. brush my teeth

2. eat pizza

3. drink milk

4. wash my hands

Let's Read

A Read and match.

1. pot   2. top   3. dot   4. octopus

B Write and circle.

1. p   a.    b.

2. d   a. ●   b.

3. o   a.   b.

4. t   a.   b. ●

✓ Parent's signature: _____

On the Beach

Where is the pot?
I want the pot.

This is my octopus!

Where is the top?
I want the top.

What is it? It's a dot.
Look at the dots.

A Trace and write.

What's your favorite color?

Blue. What about you?

I like green.

B Unscramble, write, and number.

green I like

3 I like green.

color favorite is What your

_____?

about What you Purple

_____?

Let's Learn

A Trace, match, and write.

1. a frog

2. _____

3. a dog

4. _____

birds

rabbits

_____

_____

B Write.

1. I like rabbits.

2. _____.

3. _____.

4. _____.

5. _____.

6. _____.

C Write and circle.

1. What do you like?

   I like (frogs.)
            birds.

2. _____ ?

   I like birds.
            rabbits.

3. _____ ?

   I like turtles.
            rabbits.

D Trace and write.

What do you like?

I like _____.

What do you like?

I like _____.

Let's Learn More

A Unscramble, write, and match.

1. noil

   a lion •

2. yonmek

   a •

3. frigeaf

   a •

4. thelepan

   an •

• e

• lions

• m

• g

B Write.

1.

   I like lions.
   I don't like bears.

2.

   giraffes.
   monkeys.

3.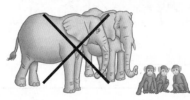

C Write.

1. Do you like lions?

    No, I don't.

2. _____ ?

    Yes, I do.

3. _____ ?

    No, I don't.

D Look and write.

rabbit   fish   lion   goat

1.

feed a _____

2.

pet a _____

3.

see a _____

4.

hear a _____

Let's Read

Phonics

A Circle.

1.

   p   (u)   t
   b   o   p
   (t)   a   (b)

2.

   b   u   t
   p   o   d
   d   i   g

   Uu

3.

   p   a   t
   c   o   p
   t   u   g

B Write and match.

| bug | umbrella | tub | cup |

1.   •   • b_____

2.  •   • u_____

3.   •   • t_____

4.   •   • c_____

70 Unit 8 Animals

✓ Parent's signature:_____

On the Playground

Oh, no!
Where is my bug?

There it is. It's on the cup.
I like bugs!

Is it on the umbrella?
No, it isn't.

Is it under the tub?
No, it isn't.

Let's Review ✓

A Read and match.

1. Do you like lions? •   • Yes, I do. I want an orange.

2. What do you want? •   • I want pizza.

3. Do you want ice cream? •   • Yes, I do. I like lions.

4. What do you like? •   • I like monkeys.

5. Do you want an orange? •   • No, I don't. I want pizza.

B Look and write.

1. I like giraffes.

2. _____ bears.

3. _____ elephants.

4. _____ lions.

C Look and check.

1.
- [ ] pizza
- [ ] chicken
- [✓] a salad
- [✓] a sandwich
- [ ] an egg

2.
- [ ] a milkshake
- [ ] milk
- [ ] a soda
- [ ] water
- [ ] juice

3.
- [ ] cake
- [ ] fish
- [ ] pizza
- [ ] ice cream
- [ ] an orange

4.
- [ ] bread
- [ ] an apple
- [ ] rice
- [ ] a banana
- [ ] a cookie

D Unscramble, write, and match.

1. rkidn kmli

drink milk

2. shaw ym dansh

3. shurb ym ehtet

4. defe a shif

Parent's signature:

My Picture Dictionary

Draw, color and write.

A

Andy

an apple

B

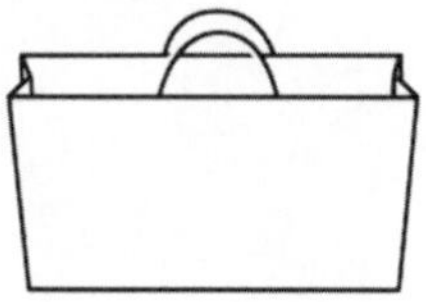

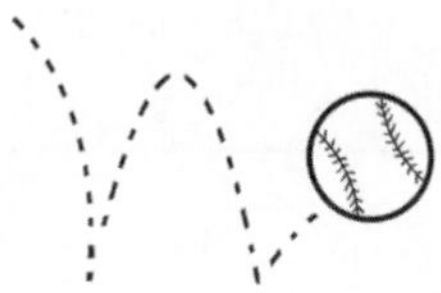

black

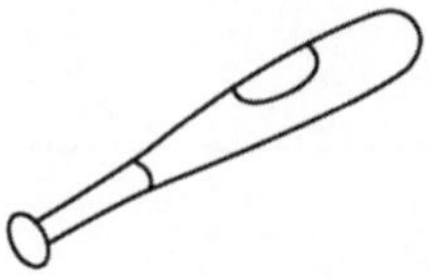

C

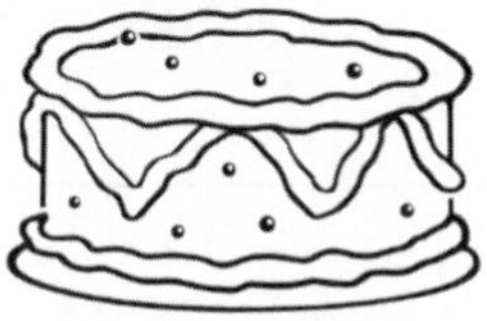

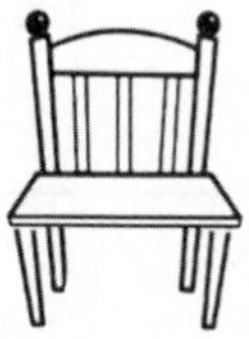

a circle

crayons

D

_____

_____

a duck

E

an egg

_____

an elephant

_____

F

_____

_____

_____

_____

G

a girl

_____

green

markers

me

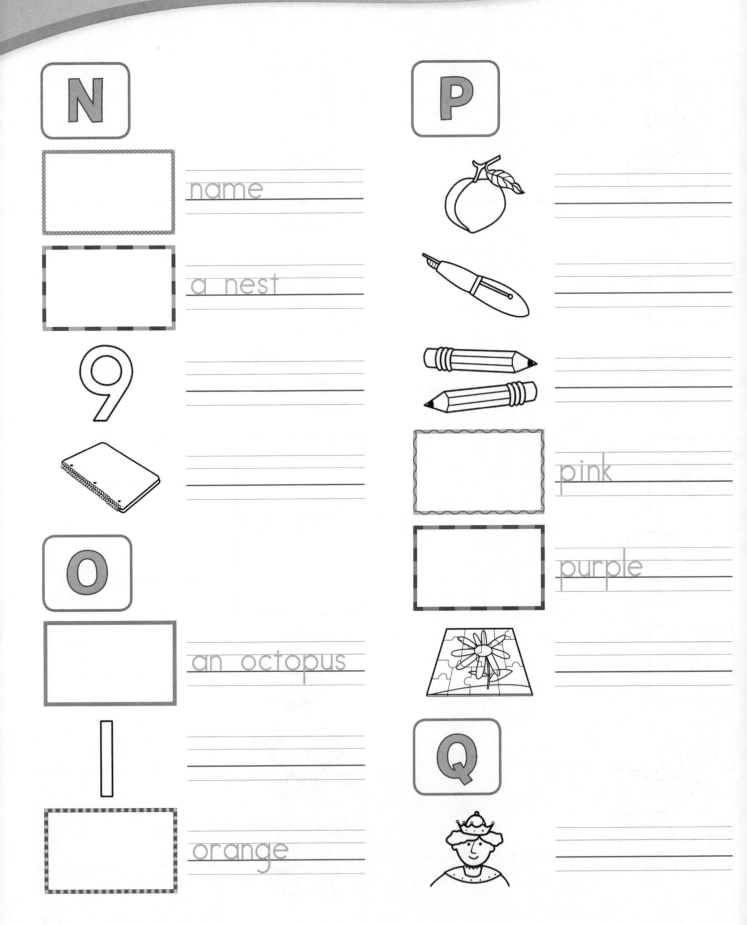

N

name

a nest

O

an octopus

orange

P

pink

purple

Q

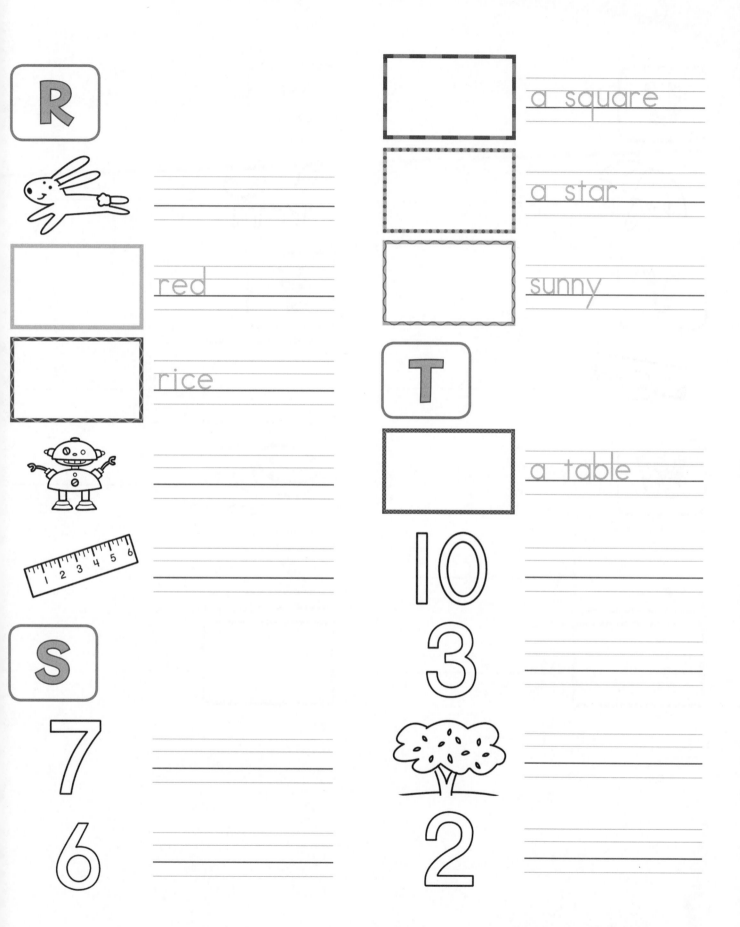

R

red

rice

a square

a star

sunny

T

a table

S

7

6

10

3

2

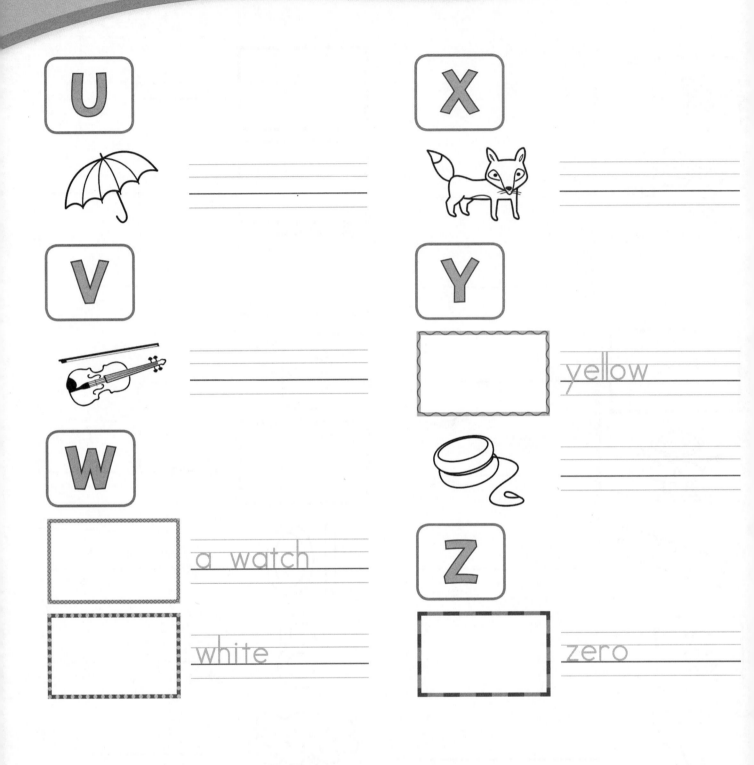

U

V

W

a watch

white

X

Y

yellow

Z

zero

✓ Parent's
signature:_____